THE NHL: HISTORY AND HEROES

PHILADELPHIA FLYERS

Published by Creative Education
P.O. Box 227, Mankato, Minnesota 56002
Creative Education is an imprint of The Creative Company.

DESIGN AND PRODUCTION BY **ZENO DESIGN**

Printed in the United States of America

PHOTOGRAPHS BY Alamy (Andre Jenny), Corbis (Bettmann), Getty Images (Steve
Bebineau/NHLI, Brian Bahr, Al Bello/Allsport, Denis Brodeur/NHLI, Bruce Bennett Studios,
Scott Cunningham, Melchior DrGiacomo, Robert Laberge/Allsport, Mitchell Layton/NHLI,
Jim McIsaac, NHLI, Ron & Patty Thomas, Brian Winkler), Hockey Hall of Fame (Imperial
Oil-Turofsky)

LIBRARY OF CONGRESS CATALOGING-IN-PUBLICATION DATA

Goodman, Michael E.
The story of the Philadelphia Flyers / by Michael E. Goodman.
p. cm. — (The NHL: history and heroes)
Includes index
ISBN 978-1-58341-620-4
1. Philadelphia Flyers (Hockey team)—History—Juvenile literature. I. Title. II. Series.

GV848.P48G66 2008
796.962'640974811—dc22   2007006951

First Edition

9 8 7 6 5 4 3 2 1

COVER: Center Daniel Briere

MICHAEL E. GOODMAN

THE NHL: HISTORY AND HEROES

PHILADELPHIA

FLYERS

IT HAS BEEN NEARLY SEVEN YEARS SINCE THE PHILADELPHIA FLYERS HAVE WON A GAME IN BOSTON GARDEN, THE BOSTON BRUINS' HOME ARENA. TONIGHT, IN GAME 2 OF THE 1974 STANLEY CUP FINALS, THEY ARE DETERMINED TO END THE DROUGHT. BUT THE BRUINS ARE READY FOR THE CHALLENGE. THEY JUMP OUT TO A 2–0 LEAD AND ARE STILL ON TOP, 2–1, WITH LESS THAN A MINUTE TO GO IN THE GAME. PHILLY MAKES A LINE CHANGE AND LAUNCHES A DESPERATE ATTACK ON THE BRUINS' GOAL. AMID THE CRASH OF BODIES, FLYERS DEFENSEMAN

FLYERS

ANDRE DUPONT OUTMANEUVERS BOSTON GOALIE GILLES GILBERT TO TIE THE GAME AND SEND IT INTO SUDDEN-DEATH OVERTIME. TWELVE MINUTES INTO OVERTIME, PHILADELPHIA'S STAR CENTER, BOBBY CLARKE, LEADS ANOTHER CHARGE AND SLAPS THE PUCK PAST GILBERT FOR THE GAME-WINNER, BREAKING THE BOSTON HEX AT LAST. TEN DAYS LATER, THE FLYERS WILL CLOSE OUT THE SERIES IN THEIR HOME ARENA, THE SPECTRUM, TO CAPTURE THE FIRST STANLEY CUP IN FRANCHISE HISTORY.

A FLYING START

THE CITY OF PHILADELPHIA, PENNSYLVANIA, was founded as a Quaker settlement along the Atlantic coast about 80 miles (129 km) south of New York City. Its founder, Englishman William Penn, gave it a Greek name meaning "brotherly love," and Philadelphia served as a model for religious tolerance in the American colonies. It quickly grew to become the largest city in the colonies and America's political center. On July 4, 1776, Philadelphia served as the birthplace of a new nation when the Declaration of Independence was signed in Independence Hall.

Philadelphia is rich in both sports and American history, home to the famous Liberty Bell and Independence Hall (visible in background).

In 1930, another group of Quakers arrived when the Pittsburgh Pirates franchise of the National Hockey League (NHL) was relocated to Philadelphia and renamed the Quakers. That club did poorly on the ice and at the ticket office and soon went out of business. For the next 30 years, Philadelphia hockey fans had to settle for rooting for a series of minor-league hockey teams.

Then, in 1967, the NHL decided to expand from a 6-team to a 12-team league and granted Philadelphia one of the new franchises. In a fan poll held to choose a name for the club, "Flyers"—a name fans felt suitably conveyed the motion and excitement of a professional hockey team—won out over such entries as "Huskies," "Blizzards," "Ice Caps," and "Knights." A new logo was designed featuring a flying "P" surrounding a bright orange hockey puck. Flyers' uniforms would feature that logo for more than 40 years.

The Flyers lost their NHL debut on the road in October 1967 to the California Seals but quickly bounced back, winning their home opener at The Spectrum eight days later. Led by center Andre LaCroix and wings Gary Dornhoefer and Leon Rochefort, the Flyers played solid team hockey, especially at home. Then, on March 1, 1968, the roof literally fell in when a fierce winter storm caused the ceiling of The Spectrum to collapse. The Flyers were forced to play most of their remaining "home" games in Quebec City in Canada, far from

FLYERS

Philly's Second Chance

BEFORE THE FLYERS JOINED THE NHL in 1967, Philadelphia hockey fans had cheered for a series of minor-league teams and one very poor NHL club—the Philadelphia Quakers, which finished with a league-worst 4–36–4 record in its one big-league season (1930–31). The Quakers quickly disbanded, but Philadelphia fans hoped for a second chance. They got their wish, thanks in large part to the efforts of Ed Snider, an executive with the Philadelphia Eagles pro football team. In 1964, Snider was attending a basketball game in Boston when he noticed a long line of hockey fans queuing up to buy tickets for an upcoming Boston Bruins game. Snider had heard that the NHL was thinking of expanding, and he saw the potential for a successful moneymaking venture if he could build a new arena in Philly and secure an expansion franchise for his city. Snider's ownership group impressed NHL officials and beat out a strong bid from a group in Baltimore, Maryland, to become part of the league. By the fall of 1967, The Spectrum, a new, state-of-the-art arena in Philadelphia, opened its doors, and the Flyers began making sports history in the City of Brotherly Love.

Philadelphia. Still, the team finished the year with a respectable 31–32–11 record to lead the West Division—made up of the league's six new teams—and earn a postseason berth. The Flyers' hustling style of play and never-say-die attitude quickly captured the hearts of Philadelphia fans. That style and attitude would carry the team far, as the feisty Flyers would reach the playoffs in 20 of their first 22 seasons.

The Flyers struggled the next two seasons, but the club's fortunes were about to change, thanks to the 1969 arrival of 20-year-old rookie center Bobby Clarke from tiny Flin Flon, Manitoba. A number of teams had passed on Clarke in the NHL Draft, believing he was too small (5-foot-10 [178 cm] and 180 pounds [82 kg]) and wouldn't be able to overcome the effects of diabetes, a disease that affects the body's blood sugar levels. The fiery Clarke quickly proved his critics wrong. In the 1970–71 season, he scrapped and hustled his

Bobby Clarke CENTER

Bobby Clarke played center on the ice and was in the middle of most of the Flyers' biggest successes for more than 30 years. Clarke starred for 15 seasons as a player in Philadelphia and was team captain when the Flyers won Stanley Cups in 1974 and 1975. He then spent more than 18 years building the team as its president and general manager. A talented scorer and passer with a blazing left-handed shot, Clarke was also one of the game's toughest defensive forwards. He was famous for his hard checks, which rattled opponents and knocked out more than a dozen of his own teeth.

FLYERS SEASONS: 1969–84
HEIGHT: 5-10 (178 cm)
WEIGHT: 180 (82 kg)

- 358 career goals
- 852 career assists
- 3-time Hart Trophy winner (as league MVP)
- Hockey Hall of Fame inductee (1987)

Known for his (eventually almost toothless) smile and aggressive body checking, Bobby Clarke became a Flyers icon and a nine-time NHL All-Star.

way to 63 points (goals plus assists). Two seasons later, Clarke rose to elite status in the NHL, piling up 104 points and earning the Hart Trophy as the league's Most Valuable Player (MVP).

The Flyers began to develop several other outstanding players as well. Wingers Rick MacLeish and Bill Barber, along with defenseman Joe Watson, helped the Flyers build momentum in the early '70s. Philadelphia's victory totals rose dramatically, going from 17 in Clarke's rookie year to 37 in 1972–73. The Flyers were on the verge of great things, and they knew it. "We've got a lot of the pieces here to win a championship," said Clarke. "We just have to find the edge that will take us to the top."

"There is no denying the tremendous bond that exists among the players from those years. It will never be broken. We won together. We sacrificed for each other, whatever it took."

PHILADELPHIA CENTER OREST KINDRACHUK,
ON THE 1970S FLYERS

12

FLYERS

Clarke vs. Diabetes

BOBBY CLARKE HAD ALL OF THE TOOLS TO be an outstanding professional hockey player—strong legs, quick reflexes, a powerful slap shot, and great leadership ability. Yet he almost didn't get a chance to play in the NHL. At age 13, Clarke was diagnosed with diabetes. People with this condition, called diabetics, can lose coordination or even suffer seizures when their blood sugar level drops too low. Clarke's disease deterred many teams from selecting him in the NHL Draft, but not the Flyers, who made Clarke their second pick in 1969. Philadelphia coaches became nervous, however, when the young star suffered two serious seizures during his first training camp because he didn't eat enough breakfast before workouts. Fortunately, assistant coach Frank Lewis came up with a solution: he developed a special regimen that Clarke would follow throughout his career. He would drink a bottle of soda filled with three spoonfuls of sugar before a game, have a bottle of orange juice at each intermission, and munch on candy bars during a game if his blood sugar level fell because of exertion. The regimen worked perfectly, and Clarke missed very few of his team's games during his 15-year career in Philadelphia.

BROAD STREET BULLIES

ALL OF THE PIECES CAME TOGETHER IN Philadelphia in the early 1970s, and the Flyers turned into a championship-caliber team. The secret to their success was a combination of aggressive play on the ice, outstanding goaltending, and inspiration from their innovative new coach, Fred Shero.

Hired in 1971, Shero seemed an odd fit as a hockey coach. Quiet and with the appearance of a college professor, Shero was known to quote classic literature and write odd inspirational phrases on the locker-room blackboards. Because he had a tendency to drift off into thought, Shero was nicknamed "Freddie the Fog." Shero stressed the importance of working

FLYERS

The rough-and-tumble Flyers, shown here in a brawl with the New York Islanders, rose quickly in the NHL standings in the early 1970s.

hard in practice as well as in games and making a serious commitment to winning. "Success is not the result of spontaneous combustion," the coach was fond of saying. "You must first set yourself on fire."

The style of play in the NHL during the 1970s was very physical, and fights were a common occurrence. Every team was tough, but Shero's Flyers were the toughest. The hard-hitting line of center Orest Kindrachuk and wings Dave "The Hammer" Schultz and Don "Big Bird" Saleski set records for penalty minutes and helped the Flyers earn the nickname "The Broad Street Bullies" (Broad Street being the street on which The Spectrum was located). Philadelphia fans of all ages loved their "Bullies." Saleski got his unusual nickname from a young fan who commented to his parents during pre-game warm-ups that the long-legged winger with the curly hair resembled the *Sesame Street* character. Some other youngsters nicknamed the often-belligerent Schultz "Oscar the Grouch," after another *Sesame Street* resident.

"I was 14 when I lost my front teeth. The main thing was, we won that game, so I was the happiest. You hate to lose your teeth and the game, too."

PHILADELPHIA WING BILL BARBER

16

FLYERS

Skating in a Flyers sweater for eight seasons, Don "Big Bird" Saleski netted his share of goals but was better known for his rugged defense.

In 1973–74, the Flyers muscled their way to a 50–16–12 record. In the play-offs, the team rode the hot goaltending of Bernie Parent all the way to the Stanley Cup Finals, where it met the mighty Boston Bruins. The series was a physical struggle, with both teams taking their lumps. Philadelphia won three of the first five games and needed just one more victory for the championship. Playing on home ice, Parent and the Flyers stonewalled the Bruins 1–0 to become the first of the six 1967 expansion teams to claim the Stanley Cup.

The Flyers focused less on bullying and more on scoring the next season after acquiring wing Reggie Leach. Known for his thunderous slap shot, Leach notched 45 goals playing with Clarke and Barber on the team's top line. "Leach can score while you blink," said Montreal Canadiens All-Star forward Bob Gainey. "He's hard to cover because once he touches the puck, he shoots it on the net."

Bill Barber WING

When the Flyers picked Bill Barber seventh overall in the 1972 NHL Draft, they knew they were getting a great scorer. But Barber turned out to be just as solid when checking opponents or setting up scoring opportunities for teammates on the power play. A natural center, Barber was switched to wing by coach Fred Shero to play alongside Bobby Clarke. Shero later added Reggie Leach to the high-scoring pair to form the "LCB" line that helped lead the Flyers to two Stanley Cups. "I think that was about the best line in history," said Montreal Canadiens coach Scotty Bowman.

FLYERS SEASONS: 1972–84
HEIGHT: 6-0 (183 cm)
WEIGHT: 195 (88 kg)

- 420 career goals
- 463 career assists
- 7-time All-Star
- Hockey Hall of Fame inductee (1990)

Known for his great natural strength, Bill Barber scored 40 or more goals every season from 1977–78 to 1980–81 before knee injuries ended his career.

With Leach aboard, the offensive-minded Flyers rolled to another Stanley Cup in 1975, this time beating the Buffalo Sabres in the Finals. "It's tough to win one championship," said Clarke. "But to go back-to-back puts us in the history books."

The Flyers hoped to make even more history the next season by capturing a third straight Cup. They came close. The "LCB" line, featuring Leach, Clarke, and Barber, established a new NHL record for goals by a single line with 141 (Leach had 61, Clarke 30, and Barber 50), and Clarke captured the last of his three career Hart Trophies. But the Flyers' championship reign ended when the Montreal Canadiens tamed the Bullies, toppling Philadelphia in a four-game Stanley Cup Finals sweep.

"I had minor-league clubs that had more real ability than [the 1974–76 Flyers], but I never had a team with this much courage, discipline, and spirit."

PHILADELPHIA COACH FRED SHERO

20

FLYERS

Stanley Cup Lucky Charm

DURING THEIR STANLEY CUP RUNS IN 1974 and 1975, the Flyers had a secret weapon who didn't wear skates or hold a stick. That "weapon" was Kate Smith, a singer famous for her recording of "God Bless America." When the recording was first played before a Flyers home game in December 1969, Philly beat the Toronto Maple Leafs. So, team management decided to play the recording more often, and the Flyers usually won on those nights. Smith loved the attention that she was getting as the team's lucky charm and agreed to perform the song live on May 19, 1974, when the Flyers faced the Boston Bruins with a chance to capture their first Stanley Cup. Smith was in great voice that night, and the Flyers skated brilliantly for a 1–0, Cup-clinching victory. When Philly needed some extra help to defeat the New York Islanders in Game 7 of the conference finals the next season, Smith agreed to make another live appearance. The result was a 4–1 Flyers win. The luck wore off in 1976, however, when not even Smith's vocals could help the Flyers avoid a Cup Finals sweep at the hands of the Montreal Canadiens.

PATRICK DIVISION POWERHOUSE

AS THE 1970S WORE ON, THE FLYERS KEPT the core of their championship teams intact and added firepower in the form of bruising wing Paul Holmgren and center Mel Bridgman to help the team stay near the top of the Patrick Division in the Campbell Conference (the NHL was split into two new conferences—Campbell and Wales—in 1974). Unfortunately for Philadelphia fans, the Flyers of the late '70s and early '80s were overshadowed by two of the greatest dynasties in NHL history—the Montreal Canadiens (who won four straight Stanley Cups from 1976 to 1979) and the New York Islanders (who won four straight Cups from 1980 to 1983).

In 1979–80, the Flyers had their best chance to topple one of the big powers. During the regular season, they established a new NHL record by going 35 games without a loss (25–0–10) and were favored to

Called aggressive by teammates and a goon by opponents, Paul Holmgren was a tough enforcer who later served as a Flyers coach.

win another championship. Philly knocked off the Edmonton Oilers, New York Rangers, and Minnesota North Stars in the first three rounds of the playoffs to reach the Stanley Cup Finals opposite the Islanders. New York proved too tough, however, capturing the series four games to two. "Looking back, that was the last hurrah for Bobby, Reggie, and all those guys from the Bullies," said Flyers center Ken Linseman. "I was 22, and I thought it was the beginning of something. Really, it was the beginning of the end."

Over the next few seasons, the Flyers experienced a major turnover of personnel. Most of the players from the championship years retired or were traded away. Three of those stars—Bobby Clarke, Bill Barber, and Bernie Parent—would later be inducted into the Hockey Hall of Fame. Clarke remained an important part of the Flyers even after retirement, serving as the team's general manager and later its president. He would help build and strengthen the franchise for most of the next two decades.

John LeClair WING

Vermont-born John LeClair's size, power, and surprising scoring touch helped turn the Flyers into big winners in the late 1990s and early 2000s. He arrived in Philadelphia along with Eric Desjardins in one of the greatest trades in franchise history. Teaming with Eric Lindros and Mikael Renberg on the "Legion of Doom" line, LeClair terrorized opponents with his powerful shot and his solid fore-checking and recorded three consecutive seasons of 50-plus goals. Positive things happened for Philadelphia when LeClair was playing, and he earned two NHL Plus/Minus Awards (meaning his team scored more goals than it gave up when he was on the ice).

FLYERS SEASONS: 1994–2004
HEIGHT: 6-3 (190.5 cm)
WEIGHT: 230 (104 kg)

- 406 career goals
- 413 career assists
- 5-time All-Star
- 2-time member of the U.S. Olympic hockey team

A key cog in the Flyers machine that won two Stanley Cups, star goalie Bernie Parent brought his great career to a close in 1979.

Clarke engineered several key trades and promoted talented players from the minor leagues to help the Flyers remain a dominant force in the Patrick Division in the early '80s. Heady defenseman Mark Howe and acrobatic goalie Pelle Lindbergh joined the club to anchor the defense, while wingers Rick Tocchet and Tim Kerr keyed an offense that played with the same bone-rattling, hardworking style to which Philly fans had grown accustomed.

> "We take the shortest route to the puck and arrive in ill humor."
>
> PHILADELPHIA CENTER BOBBY CLARKE

At 6-foot-3 (190.5 cm) and 225 pounds (102 kg), Kerr was a mountain of a man known to anchor himself in front of the opposing team's goal and use his strength and quick hands to collect loose pucks and deposit them in the net. From 1983–84 to 1988–89, he scored 48 or more goals in a season five times. "Kerr is an absolute load," said Pittsburgh Penguins defenseman Paul Coffey. "He drops that big behind of his in front of the net, and you need a bulldozer to root him out of there."

The Flyers rode Kerr's scoring and the remarkable goaltending of Lindbergh to a 53–20–7 record in 1984–85. Philadelphia then powered its way to the Stanley Cup Finals to take on the defending champion Edmonton Oilers. The Flyers dominated Game 1, but the Oilers regrouped to capture the next four games and win the Cup. Sadly, the Flyers suffered a worse loss early the next season. Lindbergh, the 26-year-old goalie who had won the Vezina Trophy

Mel Bridgman

COMING OUT OF TRAINING CAMP BEFORE the 1979–80 season, the Flyers hoped to get off to a strong start. But not many hockey experts or fans could have predicted just how spectacular a start the team would make. After splitting their first two contests, the Flyers did not lose again for nearly three months. The club earned at least one point (two points for a win and one for a tie) in every game between October 14, 1979, and January 6, 1980. When "The Streak" finally ended, the Flyers' record stood at 25–1–10. The club's 35-game unbeaten stretch was the longest ever for a professional team in any sport in North America. By season's end, the Flyers' record stood at a league-best 48–12–20, and they were a favorite to capture another Stanley Cup. The Flyers reached the Finals but fell to the Islanders, who were beginning a four-year championship run. Philadelphia's team captain during The Streak season was forward Mel Bridgman, and the scoring leaders were Reggie "The Rifle" Leach and young wing Ken Linseman, who earned the nickname "The Rat" because he could scamper across the ice so quickly and drive opponents crazy.

as the league's top netminder in 1984–85, died in a car accident.

The Lindbergh tragedy haunted the team for a while, but the Flyers pulled together and, led by rookie goalie Ron Hextall, reached the Stanley Cup Finals again in 1987 for another showdown with Edmonton. The Oilers got off to a quick start, winning three of the first four contests. Then, assuming an Oilers victory the next night, Edmonton's mayor announced plans for a championship victory parade. Incensed, Flyers coach Mike Keenan had the Stanley Cup brought into the Philly dressing room before Game 5 to inspire his club. The ploy worked, as the Flyers rallied to win the next two games, only to fall in Game 7. Hextall played magnificently in the final three contests, stopping 101 of 109 shots on goal, and even in defeat was awarded the Conn Smythe Trophy as playoffs MVP.

Mark Howe DEFENSEMAN

The son of legendary hockey great Gordie Howe, Mark Howe began his professional career in the World Hockey Association on a line with his father and brother Marty. After the trio moved to the NHL in 1979, Mark made another big switch—from wing to defenseman. Utilizing the stick-handling and passing skills he had developed as a forward, Howe became one of the top-scoring back-liners in the league and three times was runner-up for the Norris Trophy as the NHL's best defenseman. During his 10 seasons in Philadelphia, Howe anchored the club's penalty-killing team and specialized in scoring short-handed goals.

FLYERS SEASONS: 1982–92
HEIGHT: 5-11 (180 cm)
WEIGHT: 190 (86 kg)

- 197 career goals
- 545 career assists
- 4-time All-Star
- U.S. Hockey Hall of Fame inductee (2003)

Strapping wing Tim Kerr scored an NHL-record 34 power-play goals in 1985–86, including 3 in a single period (also a league record).

LINDROS AND THE LEGION OF DOOM

IN 1990, THE FLYERS FOUND THEMSELVES in an unfamiliar position—out of the playoffs for the first time in 18 years. Injuries and age had taken their toll on the team. The playoff drought continued through the 1993–94 season, but by then, the Flyers had a new star in town. On June 30, 1992, Philadelphia made one of the biggest trades in NHL history, sending Ron Hextall, the rights to five top prospects, two first-round draft picks, and $15 million to the Quebec Nordiques for the rights to rookie center Eric Lindros.

30

FLYERS

Although his later seasons were marred by concussions and discontent, Eric Lindros was a dominant force early in his Philadelphia career.

At 6-foot-4 (193 cm) and 240 pounds (109 kg), Lindros represented the new wave of power players in hockey. Skilled and fast enough to weave his way through defenders yet strong enough to blast right through them, Lindros was the biggest talent to enter the NHL in years. The Flyers added more size with 6-foot-2 (188 cm) and 210-pound (95 kg) wing Mikael Renberg in 1993 and 6-foot-3 (190.5 cm) and 230-pound (104 kg) wing John LeClair in 1994. Together, the imposing trio became a scoring machine that left opponents beaten and bruised. By the end of the 1994–95 season, the Flyers were back in the playoffs as leader of the Atlantic Division in the newly created Eastern Conference, and the line of LeClair, Lindros, and Renberg had earned the ominous nickname the "Legion of Doom." "It would be different if they were just big, or fast, or good around the net," said St. Louis Blues goaltender Grant Fuhr. "But all three of them can do it all."

Eric Desjardins DEFENSEMAN

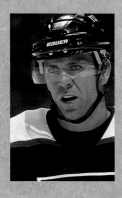

Eric Desjardins's career took a major upward turn when he was traded from the Montreal Canadiens to the Flyers in 1995. He quickly earned a reputation as both a scoring threat and a tough-as-nails checker. He also established himself as a team leader on and off the ice and was named team captain in 1999. "Desjardins was what everybody believes an athlete should be," said general manager Bobby Clarke. "He put everything in his life into the sport." The Flyers won four Atlantic Division titles and never finished lower than second with Desjardins on the roster.

FLYERS SEASONS: 1995–2006
HEIGHT: 6-1 (180 cm)
WEIGHT: 205 (93 kg)

- 136 career goals
- 439 career assists
- 3-time All-Star
- First NHL defenseman to score a hat trick (at least three goals) in a Stanley Cup Finals game

A standout from Sweden, Mikael Renberg started his Philadelphia career with a bang, setting a team rookie record with 38 goals in 1993–94.

Philadelphia's return to prominence peaked during the 1996–97 season, when the Legion of Doom produced 104 goals and 131 assists, thrilling home-town crowds in the newly built CoreStates Center (later renamed the Wachovia Center). In the postseason, the Flyers quickly won three playoff series and reached the Stanley Cup Finals for the seventh time in franchise history. Then their winning touch evaporated, as the Detroit Red Wings swept the series to capture the Cup. Following the season, Flyers management engineered several key trades in an effort to build a more balanced offense.

"When Eric Lindros comes off the Flyers' bench against us, I shake—every time. That doesn't happen with anyone else."

FLORIDA PANTHERS COACH DOUG MacLEAN

The tinkering began to pay off in 1999–2000, when Philadelphia roared to a 45–25–12 record. New Flyers standouts such as big center Keith Primeau and speedy wing Simon Gagne, along with veterans Lindros, LeClair, and winger Mark Recchi, led the team to playoff wins over the Buffalo Sabres and Pittsburgh Penguins. Facing the New Jersey Devils in the Eastern Conference Finals, Philadelphia won three of the first four games before the Devils battled back to tie the series. In the first period of the deciding Game 7, Lindros was knocked out with a concussion by a brutal mid-ice check from Devils defenseman Scott Stevens. Without their star, the Flyers lost 2–1.

FLYERS

IN THE 40,218 NHL GAMES PLAYED BEFORE December 8, 1987, no goalie had ever shot a puck into the opponent's net for a goal. Many goalies had recorded an assist by sending the puck ahead to a skater streaking down the ice, but none had actually recorded a shot on goal. Then Flyers goalie Ron Hextall entered the record books by scoring in the closing seconds of a contest against the Boston Bruins. With Philly up 4–2, Boston had pulled its goalie to get an extra skater on the ice. Hextall noticed the empty Boston net and went out from his own goal to grab the loose puck and shoot it high in the air down the ice. It landed near the Boston blue line and rolled into the empty net, just inside the left post. "I was hoping to get the puck close. I shot it and saw it roll in," said Hextall. "It was a great feeling." Against all odds, Hextall would get another thrill and make hockey history again just 17 months later when he scored an empty-net goal in an 8–5 Philly victory over the Washington Capitals during the first round of the 1989 playoffs.

For Lindros, the injury was just the latest in a long series of concussions. Concerned about his health and trying to force a trade away from Philadelphia, Lindros sat out the 2000–01 season. While he was recovering, a long-simmering feud with team president Bobby Clarke boiled over. Clarke felt that Lindros needed to be tougher and play through his injuries, but Lindros was reluctant to take the risk. Before the 2001–02 season, Clarke traded Lindros to the New York Rangers for three players and a draft pick. "Eric didn't want to be in Philadelphia," said Clarke, "and I was more than happy to accommodate him."

To replace Lindros, the Flyers signed veteran center Jeremy Roenick. A six-time All-Star with the Chicago Blackhawks and Phoenix Coyotes, the high-scoring Roenick led the Flyers to another division title in 2001–02. The season came to an abrupt end, however, when Philly fell to the Ottawa Senators in the first round of the playoffs.

"Philadelphia fans are the most loyal, long-suffering, vociferous, in-the-blood, in-your-face sports fans in America."

PHILADELPHIA SPORTSWRITER GLEN MACNOW

36

FLYERS

Jeremy Roenick arrived in Philadelphia in 2001 with 13 seasons of NHL experience and quickly won over the Philadelphia faithful.

The Flyers remained a contender early in the new century, winning at least 40 games and making the playoffs every year from 1999–2000 to 2005–06.

ATLANTIC ACES

THE TEAM'S QUICK EXIT FROM THE 2002 postseason forced Clarke to make some changes at the top, replacing his former line-mate Bill Barber as coach with Ken Hitchcock, who had previously led the Dallas Stars to a Stanley Cup championship. Hitchcock looked for on-ice leadership from longtime Flyers such as Primeau and Gagne and new acquisitions such as goalie Robert Esche.

For the next two seasons, the Flyers battled the New Jersey Devils for supremacy in the Atlantic Division. In 2002–03, the Devils came out on top and eventually won the Stanley Cup, while the Flyers fell in the second round of the playoffs to the Ottawa Senators. The next season, the teams reversed positions. The Flyers got off to a great start, losing only

Ken Hitchcock established himself as a top coach in the mid-1990s, building winning records in Dallas and then Philadelphia for nine straight seasons.

3 of their first 22 games. They edged out New Jersey for the division title and then defeated their neighbors to the north in the first round of the playoffs. The Flyers kept winning behind the hot goaltending of Esche and the scoring of Roenick and Gagne to reach a Game 7 showdown in the Eastern Conference Finals against the Tampa Bay Lightning. One more victory would put them in another Stanley Cup Finals. But it was not to be. The Lightning jumped out to a 2–0 lead, and the Flyers came up short when they were able to score only one goal of their own.

Philly fans were looking forward to big things in 2004–05. Then the entire season was cancelled after owners locked out players in a major contract dispute. After the lockout was finally resolved, Clarke made big news by signing star center Peter Forsberg, a former league MVP. "We're really, really excited to have Peter here with us, and we hope he puts the finishing touches on our team," said Clarke.

Bernie Parent GOALIE

When Bernie Parent returned to Philadelphia before the 1973–74 season, it marked a turning point in franchise history. An original expansion draft selection in 1967, Parent had been traded away in 1971. Luckily, the club recognized its mistake and reacquired him three seasons later. Flyers fans were thrilled, and many decorated their cars with bumper stickers proclaiming, "Only the Lord saves more than Bernie Parent." Although average in size, Parent's stand-up technique and intense concentration helped him become a dominant netminder. He played nearly every game during the Flyers' two Stanley Cup championship seasons and was named playoffs MVP each year.

FLYERS SEASONS: 1967–71, 1973–79
HEIGHT: 5–10 (178 cm)
WEIGHT: 170 (77 kg)

- 271 career wins
- 54 career shutouts
- 2-time Vezina Trophy winner (as best goaltender)
- Hockey Hall of Fame inductee (1984)

Peter Forsberg, whom the Flyers had traded away in the blockbuster deal for Eric Lindros in 1992, made a triumphant return to Philadelphia in 2005.

Many hockey experts predicted another Stanley Cup for the rejuvenated Flyers, especially after Forsberg led them to the top of the Eastern Conference standings early in the 2005–06 season. The Flyers' top line of Forsberg, Gagne, and winger Mike Knuble quickly became one of the most potent in the NHL. Then the team was struck by a wave of injuries, including career-threatening ones to Forsberg and Gagne. Philadelphia finished the year fifth in the conference and was quickly eliminated in the playoffs. The team continued a downward spiral the following year, failing to make the playoffs for the first time in 12 years, but young stars such as goalie Antero Nittymaki and centers Mike Richards and Jeff Carter gained valuable experience for the future.

The city of Philadelphia has a long history both as the nation's birthplace and as the home of great professional franchises in hockey and other major sports. Since their founding in 1967, the Flyers have been an important part of that history, developing a tough, winning style that has captured the devotion of Philly fans and struck fear into the hearts of opponents. Today, the hockey club in the bright orange-and-black sweaters plans to continue making its opponents black and blue.

44

FLYERS

The Legion of Doom

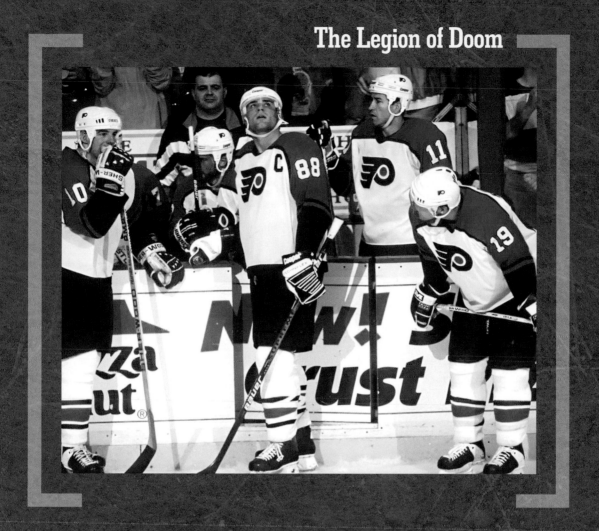

DURING THE 1994–95 SEASON, FLYERS coach Terry Murray created a new top line for the Flyers featuring center Eric Lindros and forwards John LeClair and Mikael Renberg. Individually, each player was big and strong and had impressive offensive and defensive skills. Together, they became a dominant force on the ice. The line would make rush after rush on the opponent's net and then use solid fore-checking to set up more scoring opportunities. They piled up points and helped revive the Flyers' fortunes after several subpar seasons. Philly sportswriters couldn't decide what to call the talented trio. Then, one night after the line did most of the scoring in a 7–0 rout of the Montreal Canadiens, Philly center Jim Montgomery remarked, "Those guys looked like the Legion of Doom out there tonight." Fans loved the comparison of the Flyers' stars to the cartoon supervillains who used their evil powers to take on superheroes such as Superman and Batman on television each week. Philadelphia's Legion of Doom proved to be a frightening force against their opponents. The line led the Flyers to their first division title in eight years and all the way to the 1995 Eastern Conference Finals.

Fred Shero COACH

With his tinted glasses and mild manners, Fred Shero didn't look like the architect of the Broad Street Bullies. But Shero had his tough side, too. Growing up in Winnipeg, Manitoba, Shero was a standout hockey player and boxer. After playing three unspectacular seasons with the New York Rangers, he turned to coaching, where his hockey knowledge and intellectual style proved a perfect combination. Shero was famous for his tough practices and his inspirational sayings. Before the Flyers' Stanley Cup-clinching game in 1974, Shero told his players, "Win together today, and we walk together forever." The players responded with a 1–0 victory.

FLYERS SEASONS AS COACH: 1971–78
NHL COACHING RECORD: 390–225–119
STANLEY CUP CHAMPIONSHIPS WITH PHILADELPHIA: 1974, 1975
1974 NHL COACH OF THE YEAR

FLYERS

INDEX

B

Barber, Bill 12, 16, 18, 20, 24, 40
Bridgman, Mel 22, 27
"Broad Street Bullies" 16, 24, 47

C

Carter, Jeff 44
Clarke, Bobby 5, 10, 12, 13, 18, 20, 24,
    26, 32, 36, 40, 42
Conn Smythe Trophy 28
CoreStates Center 34

D

Desjardins, Eric 24, 32
Dornhoefer, Gary 8
Dupont, Andre 5

E

Esche, Robert 40, 42

F

first season 8, 10
Forsberg, Peter 42, 44

G

Gagne, Simon 34, 40, 42, 44

H

Hart Trophy 10, 12, 20
Hextall, Ron 28, 30, 35
Hitchcock, Ken 40
Hockey Hall of Fame 10, 18, 24, 42
Holmgren, Paul 22
Howe, Mark 26, 28

K

Keenan, Mike 28
Kerr, Tim 26
Kindrachuk, Orest 12, 16
Knuble, Mike 44

L

LaCroix, Andre 8
Leach, Reggie 18, 20, 24, 27
LeClair, John 24, 32, 34, 45
"Legion of Doom" 24, 32, 34, 45
Lewis, Frank 13
Lindbergh, Pelle 26, 28
Lindros, Eric 24, 30, 32, 34, 36, 45
Linseman, Ken 24, 27

M

MacLeish, Rick 12
Montgomery, Jim 45
Murray, Terry 45

N

National Hockey League records 20, 22,
    27, 35
Nittymaki, Antero 44

P

Parent, Bernie 18, 24, 42
Philadelphia Quakers 8, 9
Pittsburgh Pirates 8
playoffs 5, 10, 18, 20, 21, 24, 26, 27, 28,
    32, 34, 35, 36, 40, 42, 44, 45
Primeau, Keith 34, 40

R

Recchi, Mark 34
Renberg, Mikael 24, 32, 45
Richards, Mike 44
Rochefort, Leon 8
Roenick, Jeremy 36, 42

S

Saleski, Don 16
Schultz, Dave 16
Shero, Fred 14, 16, 18, 20, 47
Smith, Kate 21
Snider, Ed 9
Spectrum 5, 8, 9, 16
Stanley Cup championships 5, 10, 18,
    20, 21, 42
Stanley Cup Finals 5, 18, 20, 21, 24, 26,
    27, 28, 34

T

team name 8
Tocchet, Rick 26

U

U.S. Hockey Hall of Fame 28

V

Vezina Trophy 28, 42

W

Wachovia Center 34
Watson, Joe 12

FLYERS